# SCHIRMER'S LIBRARY
## OF MUSICAL CLASSICS

Vol. 693

# THIRTY-TWO
# SONATINAS
# and RONDOS

## For the Piano

By

### CLEMENTI, KUHLAU, DUSSEK, HAYDN, MOZART, BEETHOVEN, HOFMANN, RAFF, SCHUMANN

Progressively Arranged

Fingering and Expression-Marks by
RICHARD KLEINMICHEL

ISBN 978-0-7935-4995-5

## G. SCHIRMER, Inc.

DISTRIBUTED BY

HAL•LEONARD®
CORPORATION
7777 W. BLUEMOUND RD. P.O. BOX 13819 MILWAUKEE, WI 53213

# INDEX

PAGE

BEETHOVEN, L. van    Bagatelle in C major, Op. 119, No. 7    133
"   "    Klavierstück (Piano-piece) " für Elise," in A minor    130
"   "    Rondo in C major, Op. 51, No. 1    124
"   "    Sonatina in G minor, Op. 49, No. 1    100
"   "    Sonatina in G major,   "   "   2    95
"   "    Six Variations on " Nel cor più non mi sento "    114
"   "    Six Easy Variations in G major    120
CLEMENTI, M.    Sonatina in C major, Op. 36, No. 1    1
"   "    Sonatina in G major,   "   "   2    4
"   "    Sonatina in C major,   "   "   3    8
"   "    Sonatina in G major,   "   "   5    12
"   "    Sonatina in D major   "   "   6    19
DUSSEK, J. L.    Sonatina in G major, Op. 20, No. 1    51
"   "    Sonatina in F major,   "   "   3    54
HAYDN, J.    Serenade from the F-major Quartet, Op. 3, No. 5    93
"   "    Sonata in C major    80
HOFMANN, H.    Gavotte in F major, Op. 88, No. 1    76
"   "    " In Hungarian Style," "   "   4    78
KUHLAU, F.    Rondo in A major, Op. 40, No. 2    89
"   "    Rondo in F major,   "   "   3    91
"   "    Sonatina in C major, Op. 20, No. 1    45
"   "    Sonatina in C major, Op. 55, No. 1    25
"   "    Sonatina in G major,   "   "   2    29
"   "    Sonatina in C major,   "   "   3    33
"   "    Sonatina in F major,   "   "   4    37
"   "    Sonatina in D major,   "   "   5    41
"   "    Sonatina in G major, Op. 88, No. 2    60
"   "    Sonatina in A minor,   "   "   3    64
MOZART, W. A.    Sonata in C major    69
RAFF, J.    Étude in F major    112
SCHUMANN, R.    Little Lullaby in G major, Op. 124, No. 6    107
"   "    Slumber-song in E♭ major,   "   "   16    108

# Clementi, Sonatina.

## Op. 36, Nº 1.

**Allegro.**

Printed in the U.S.A. by G. Schirmer, Inc.

**Andante.**

*dolce*

*sempre legato*

**Vivace.**

# Clementi, Sonatina.

## Op. 36, No 2.

**Allegretto.**

Allegretto.

6

Allegro.

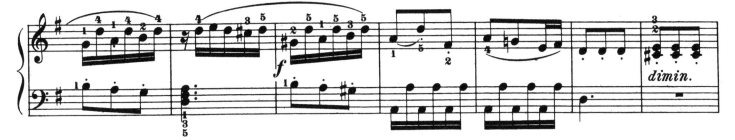

# Clementi, Sonatina.

## Op. 36, No 3.

Spiritoso.

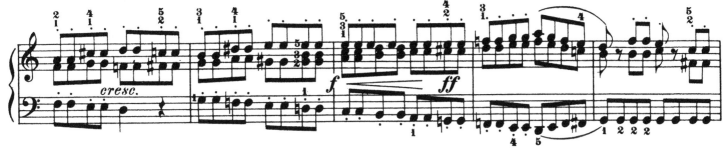

10

Un poco adagio.

Allegro.

# Clementi, Sonatina.

## Op. 36, № 5.

15600

Original Swiss Air.
Allegro moderato.

*Note.* When the turn-sign is *over* the note, the turn should always be played thus:

dolce

cresc.

f

sempre legato

p

rall.

15

15600

**Rondo.**
Allegro molto.

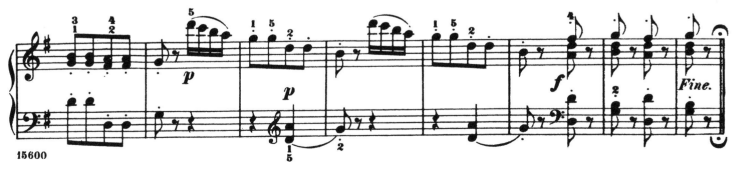

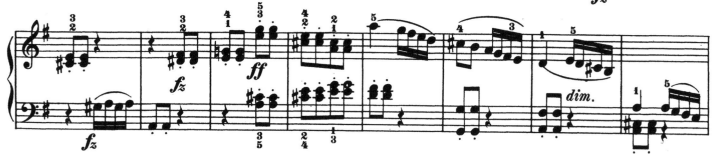

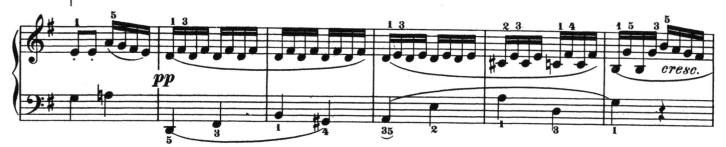

# Clementi, Sonatina.
## Op. 36, Nº 6.

Allegro con spirito.

dolce  fz  p  legato

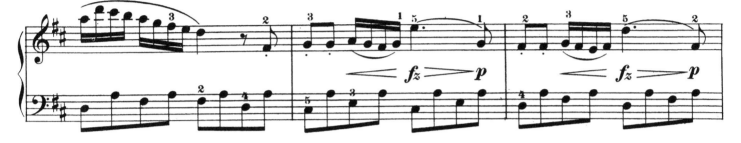

fz  p  fz  p

cresc.

f  ff

fz

fz

15600

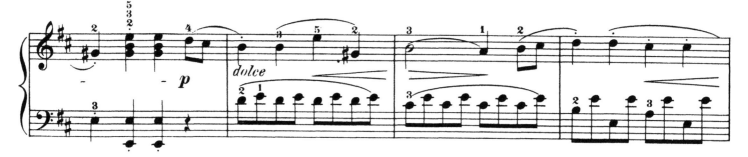

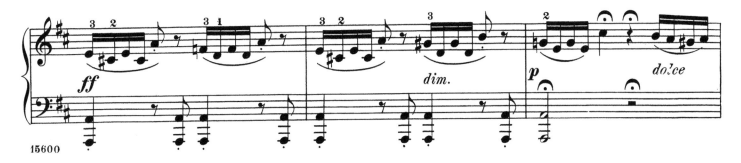

15600

**Rondo.**
Allegretto spiritoso.

24

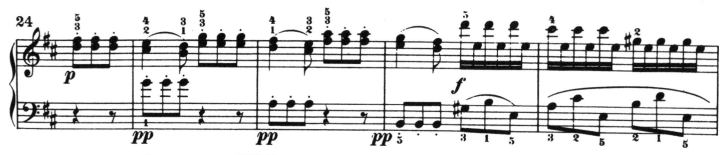

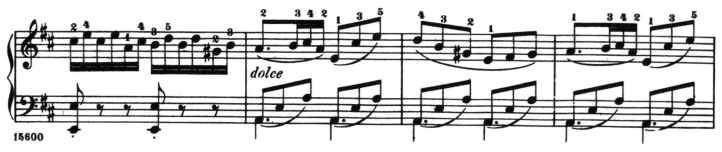

D.C. al Fine.

## Kuhlau, Sonatina.
### Op. 55, № 1.

Allegro.

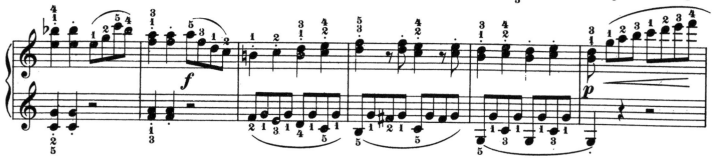

**Vivace.**

# Kuhlau, Sonatina.
## Op. 55, № 2.

30

Cantabile.

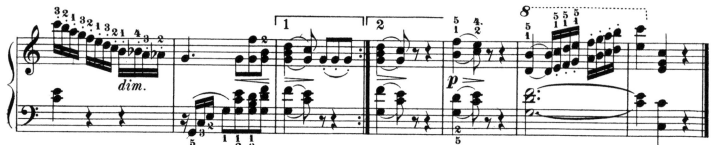

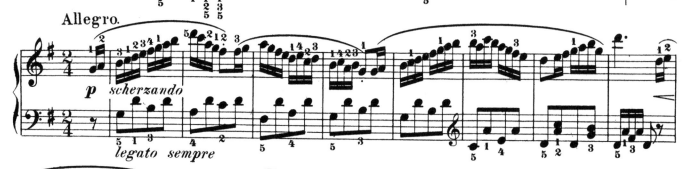

Allegro.

15600

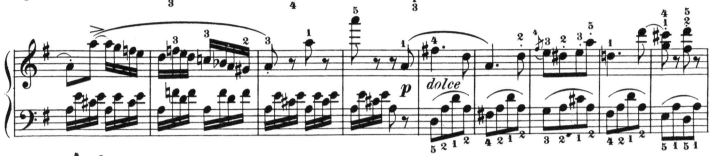

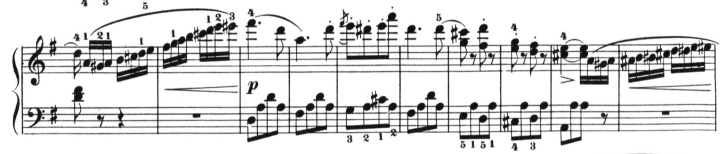

15600

*a tempo*

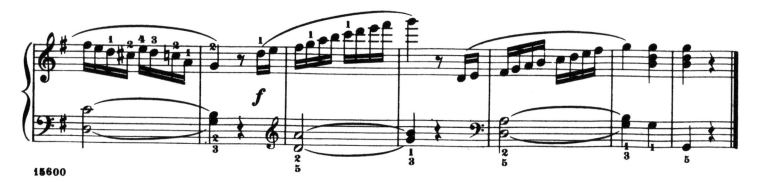

# Kuhlau, Sonatina.

## Op. 55, № 3.

Allegro con spirito.

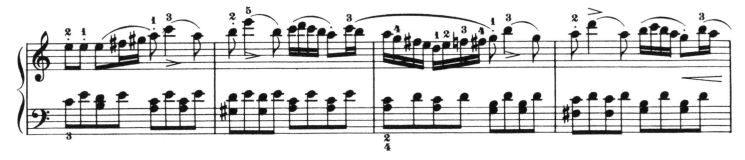

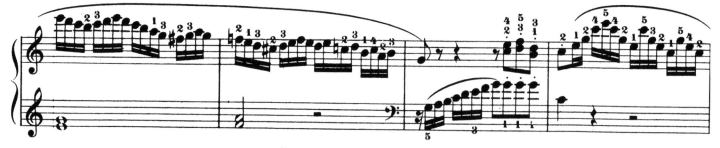

Allegretto grazioso.

15600

# Kuhlau, Sonatina.

**Op. 55, № 4.**

Allegro non tanto.

**Andantino con espressione.**

**Alla Polacca.**

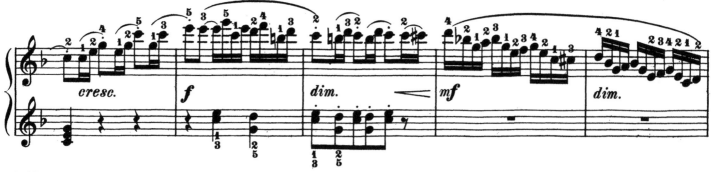

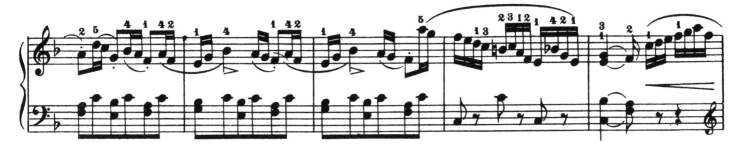

*Da capo al Segno ⊕ e poi la Coda \*)*

**Coda.**

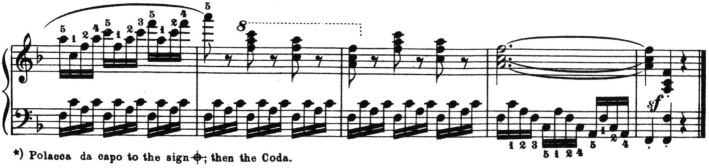

\*) Polacca da capo to the sign ⊕; then the Coda.

15660

# Kuhlau, Sonatina.
## Op. 55, № 5.

**Tempo di Marcia.**

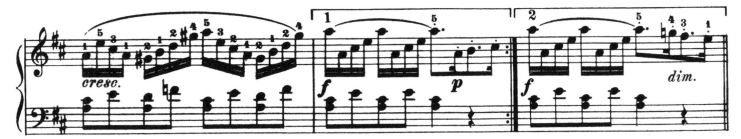

15600

Vivace assai.

*sempre legato*

15600

## Kuhlau, Sonatina.
### Op. 20, № 1.

46

Andante.

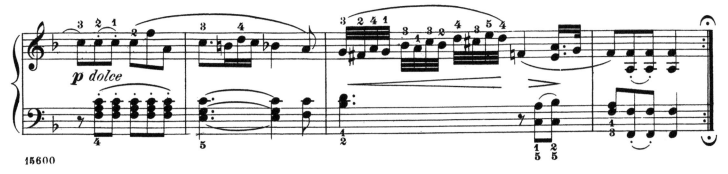

# Rondo.
### Allegro.

# Dussek, Sonatina.
## Op.20, № 1.

Allegro cantando.

**Rondo.**
Allegretto. Tempo di Menuetto.

Dussek, Sonatina.
Op. 20, № 3.

Allegro quasi presto.

## Rondo.
### Andantino.

58

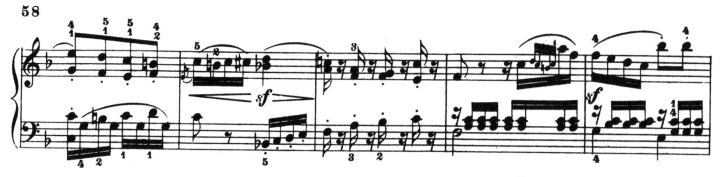

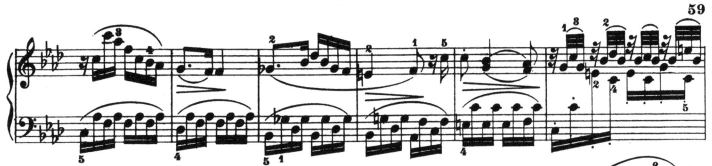

# Kuhlau, Sonatina.
## Op. 88, № 2.

Allegro assai.

61

Andante cantabile.

15600

**Rondo.**
Vivace.

# Kuhlau, Sonatina.
## Op. 88, № 3.

**Allegretto con affetto.**

15600

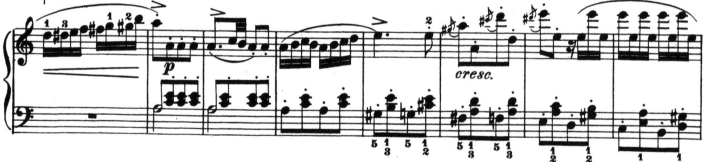

## Mozart, Sonata.

15600

Andante.

# Rondo.
## Allegretto.

15600

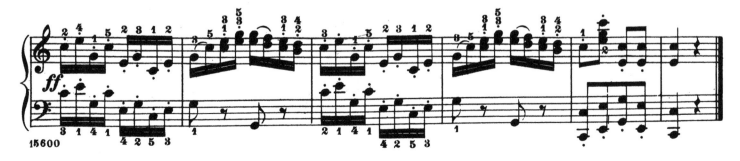

# Heinrich Hofmann.

### Stimmungsbilder. (Mood - pictures.)

**Op. 88, No 1. Gavotte.**

15600

# Heinrich Hofmann.

## Stimmungsbilder. (Mood – pictures.)

### Op. 88, № 4. Ungarisch. (In Hungarian Style.)

Allegro non troppo.

15600

# Haydn, Sonata.

**Allegro con brio.**

♦) Turn-sign <u>over</u> note always played thus:

15600

Adagio. Tempo I.

15600

84

Adagio.

*) Long (accented) appoggiatura:

15600

**Finale.**
Allegro.

# Kuhlau, Rondo.
## Op. 40, № 2.

15600

# Kuhlau, Rondo.
## Op. 40, № 3.

Allegretto grazioso.

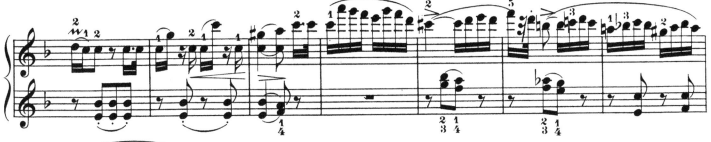

# Haydn, Serenade.

### From the F-major Quartet Op. 3, № 5.

(Long, Short and Double Appoggiaturas, Unaccented Double Appoggiatura, Trill.)

**Andante cantabile.**

# Beethoven, Sonatina.

## Op. 49, № 2.

**Allegro ma non troppo.**

15600

96

*) Long appoggiatura:

15600

**Tempo di Minuetto.**

Beethoven, Sonatina.

**Andante.**

Op. 49, № 1.

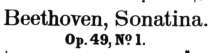

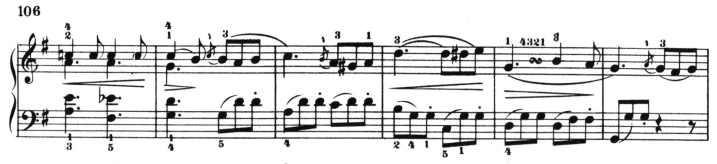

# Robert Schumann.

## Albumblätter. (Album-leaves.)

### Op.124, № 6. Wiegenliedchen. (Little Lullaby.)

Nicht schnell. (♩ = 120)
*Non allegro.*

15600

# Robert Schumann.

### Albumblätter. (Album-leaves.)

**Op. 124, № 16. Schlummerlied. (Slumber song.)**

Allegretto.($\quad$= 69)

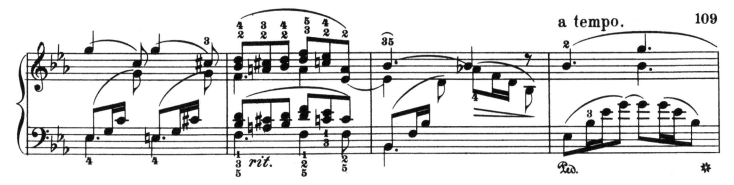

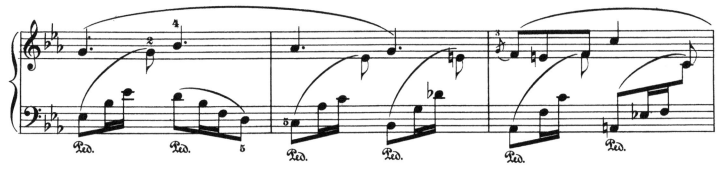

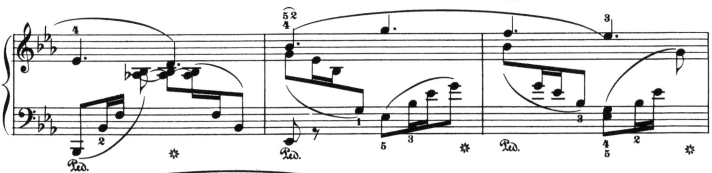

15600

a tempo.

# J. Raff, Étude.

**Allegro molto.**

# Beethoven, Six Variations.

## on the Duet "Nel cor più non mi sento," by Paisiello.

Un poco animato.

Var. III.

Minore.

Var. IV.

118 Più animato quasi Allegretto.

15600

# Beethoven, six easy variations.

Andante quasi allegretto.

Var.III.

**Minore.**
Poco sostenuto.

Var. IV.

Maggiore.

Var. V.

Var. VI.

**Coda.**

Beethoven, Rondo.
Op. 51, № 1.

Moderato e grazioso.

*) Always play the turn *over* the note thus:

15600

15600

Un poco più animato.

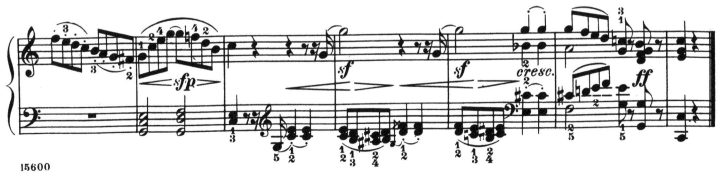

# L. van Beethoven.

### Klavierstück. (Piano-piece.)
### Für Elise. (For Eliza.)

15600

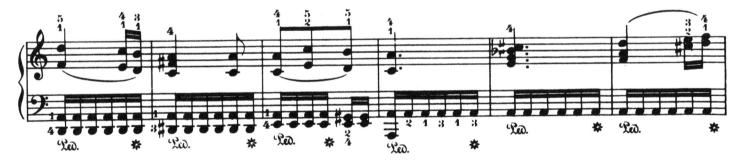

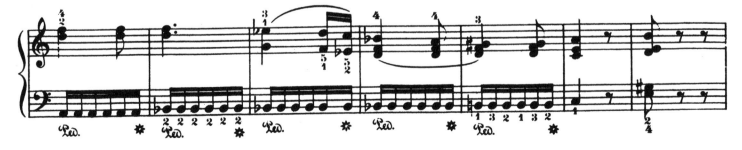

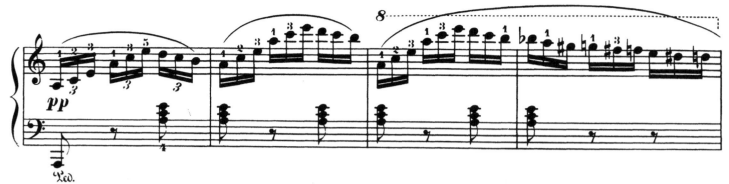

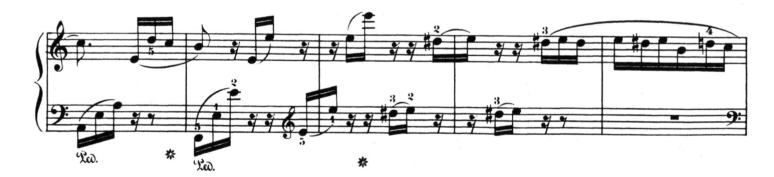

# Beethoven, Bagatelle.
## Op. 119, № 7.

Allegro ma non troppo. (♩ = 92)

*) Fingering for the trills written by Beethoven himself, according to Starke's "Pianoforte-Method" (for which this Bagatelle was written,) Vienna, 1821, the original edition of Schlesinger, Paris. 1823, and the edition of Sauer & Leidesdorf. Vienna, 1824.

15600